# Where No Window Was

by

## Ruth Roach Pierson

BuschekBooks

National Library of Canada Cataloguing in Publication Data

Pierson, Ruth Roach, 1938-
    Where no window was

Poems
ISBN 1-894543-08-4

    I. Title.

PS8581.I2815W47 2002        C811'.6        C2002-900358-X
PR9199.4.P53W47 2002

Cover image: based on *Indicator* by Elaine Whittacker, 1999, Chromagenic print (light passed through grown salt crystals, no camera or negative), 11" x 14"

Cover photo of Ruth Roach Pierson by Joan Latchford.

Printed in Canada by Hignell Book Printing, Winnipeg, Manitoba.

BuschekBooks gratefully acknowledges the support of
the Canada Council for the Arts and the Ontario
Arts Council for its publishing program.

BuschekBooks
P.O. Box 74053, 5 Beechwwod Avenue
Ottawa, Ontario  K1M 2H9
Canada
Email: buschek.books@sympatico.ca
Editor: John Buschek

ONTARIO ARTS COUNCIL
CONSEIL DES ARTS DE L'ONTARIO

The Canada Council | Le Conseil des Arts
for the Arts | du Canada

*for*

*Dwight Raymond Boyd*

A sinister spider named Ruth
set up a photography booth.
In clever disguise
she'd lure juicy flies
who too late would discover the truth.
James Marshall


The past: that's what I think about while meditating on the
pomegranates.
That's when the trouble always starts. The past is all we've
got
When we haven't yet learned how to sit and see.
Steve Orlen


"The difference [between the historian and the poet] is that
the one tells of what has happened, the other of the kinds of
things that might happen. For this reason poetry is something
more philosophical and more worthy of serious attention than
history..."
Aristotle

# *T*able of Contents

# $A$ cknowledgements

I could not have made the turn from writing academic history to writing poems without the inspiration and encouragement of a number of poet/teachers remarkable for their dedication to poetry and their pedagogic skill, most significantly Helen Humphreys, Betsy Struthers, Don McKay, Daphne Marlatt, Ken Babstock and A.F. Moritz. To the latter two I am especially indebted for the sympathetic reading and careful editing they gave to earlier stages of this manuscript.

First drafts of poems are written in solitude, but the company of others, whose opinion the poet values, is often sought in the long process of revision. Over the years I have enjoyed the benefit of responses to my poems from poetry group members with whom I have worked. Paramount among them is Patria Rivera, my most long-standing workshop mate. To her a huge thanks. Also to my fellow OISE Poets, an evolving group that has included, in addition to Patria, Stephen Gardner, Todd Engle, Tanis MacDonald, Mary Ellen Csamer, Kate Rogers, Alison Hancock and, in its most recent incarnation as the Sixth Floor Poets, Rosemary Blake, Mary Lou Soutar-Hynes, Sheila Stewart and John Oughton.

And where would I be without the support of writer/poet friends like Barbara Klar, Marlene Cookshaw, Mitch Parry, Kelley Aitken, Alayna Munce, and Susannah Smith.

My heartfelt appreciation also to the Banff Centre for the Arts and to the Sage Hill Fall Poetry Colloquium.

Above all I should like to express my deep gratitude to John Buschek, the editor/publisher of this book.

Finally my thanks to the editors of the following journals and anthologies where many of these poems, often in slightly different versions, first appeared: *Arc, The Edges of Time: A Celebration of Canadian Poetry* (Seraphim Editions, 1999), *Grain, The Literary Review of Canada, The Malahat Review, No Choice but to Trust* (UnMon America, 2000), *Not To Rest in Silence: A Celebration of People's Poetry* (UnMon Northland, 1996), *Pagitica, The Pottersfield Portfolio, PRISM International, Room of One's Own,* the League of Canadian Poets' National Poetry Contest, *Vintage 1999* and *Vintage 2000*, *Waiting for you to speak* (UnMon American 1999), and *Word: Toronto's Literary Calendar*.

# *Le dernier sommeil*

Brought up out of the museum's hidden vaults,
a mausoleum of *objets morbide* and animal dead.

Tagged, catalogued, limbs and wings trussed,
life's fuss combed out of fur and feather.
Bodies lie stiff, eye holes

stitched closed or filled
with glass marbles like mother-of-pearl
buttons on women's kid boots.

Spooky the still and jolt of Hurlbut's
juxtapositions: cat mummies,
lethal baby bottles, a bullet bra.

In one *vitrine*, albino robins,
crows. Nearby five snowy owls,
expectedly white plumed.

The skeleton specimen of a once-captive
gray gibbon poses upright,
left forelimb swung over a wire stand.

Divested of plumage, the death's head
of the sulphur-crested cockatoo
could easily be mistaken

for the common loon. How tiny
the skulls of the shrew, deer mouse,
little brown bat. Human dead

are seldom so preserved: a few
*memento mori*, wax museum replicas,
the occasional head of state

floating in formaldehyde like these bottled
fish, yellowing.  May you and I never
 be so displayed—body embalmed

or bared to the bone, arm draped
like a drunken rake's around a lamppost.

# Word Usage

*"It is hardly the sphere, Sir Godfrey, in which the dictates of Dame Fashion need be meticulously adhered to," said Dominic...*
*"I wish I could use a word like `meticulously' as a matter of course," said Gregory.*

Ivy Compton-Burnett

She sat in the room's studied
disarray, unmeticulously clad
in a ratty bathrobe of some
synthetic mix, listening
to the tinny click, click
of a yellow-bellied sapsucker's beak
against her chimney's metal flashing,
sunk in a stupor of admiration
at the morning ablutions of her cat,
the rhythmic rotation of tongue, paw,
whiskered cheek, a ritual the furred animal,
in studied disregard of the bird on the roof,
meticulously cleaves to as a navigator
adheres to his course.

# Child's Play

While he lay wheezing in a shuttered room,
she ran through the long grass,
turned cartwheels, climbed trees
and pounced—Lil' Abner's wolf girl—
on unsuspecting prey.  She could pump

the swing in the tall maple
so high the aunts and uncles feared
she'd sail away over the top,
                              but to her it was all

delirious flight from that sun-
eclipsing silhouette,
thin back bent, chest concave,
inflamed nose stuck in a book,
a chill reproach to every step,
to every breath she took with ease.

# Conceit

I don't know that there always has to be
an "I"—camera's aperture, mast
to cling to, pole to run a flag up.
Auto for the bio. No
cynosure or paparazzo darkens
a Caspar David Friedrich scene,
only the drama of oak, soaring mountain,
sky. Piet Mondrian purged his art
of all but geometry and equilibrium.
And may Saul Bellow rest assured,
the parade of pictures, that play
of light and shadow philosophers call
appearance, will soldier on after
our eyelids are weighted with coins.
What is our fear: that without an "I"
there'd be no "us," no "you"?
Or that beauty's site of being—
the "I" of the beholder—vanishes
into the eye of a passing cloud?

# Unfolding as it should

She stands astride
the Tigris and Euphrates,
her task—to unfold

the papyrus of days.  Anchored
ankle deep in black
mud, as svelte and velvety

as ambrosia, she taps fingers,
finely tapered from the unfurling
of centuries, along the rolled

end of the scroll, feeling for the weight
of momentous event or the turbulence
of volcanic sea change, imagining

the lightning, the coalescence
of that first day's particles.

# Caught

I sit in the scent of a lilac
and the shadow from a neighbour's maple,
reading a memoir by Erich Fried, about fleeing Vienna
after Hitler's *Einmarsch*, streets
scrawled with *Jude verrecke!*,
his grandmother trapped and left behind—when

a sudden gust fills the sky
with propeller blades—
little *Ausrufezeichen*—
their plummeted spinning
drawing a veil between me
and what's beyond this garden.  When I was a child

(such a different childhood!)
one upside-down shake let loose silent snow
within my grandmother's glass globe—
for an instant, I'm caught
inside the belled scene, the only sound
a whir of keys falling
onto lilac, book,
my unsleeved arm.

# *R*epeat *Performances*

1.
Evenings my parents sat out here,
watched the sun leave the river.
A kingfisher chatters, sweeping
in low, following the stream's
curve to his perch in an alder
cantilevered over the water.
There he waits, watches,
dives for his dinner.

Two end-of-the-day riparian rituals:
his, born of instinct or intelligent habit,
utilitarian; mine,
merely chosen repetition,
not unlike the act of collecting—
one more piece of art deco vaseline glass
or another 1920s fishing reel—

as though, by this proliferation of the same,
things will be kept as they were.


2.
At the edge of the crabgrass lawn
behind the house on Phinney Bay
once waded up to my chin
in a sea of swaying poppies

yet when I walk the summer streets
now I find beds
of ballooning impatiens, whole
tea parties of lacy cosmos
but only a straggle
of those childhood poppies

I still see
on a sun-drugged summer afternoon
billowing out in slow
*Elvira Madigan* motion
from black-seeded centres

floral fireworks
at eye level

as in Emil Nolde's *Großer Mohn*
I realize as I enter
his inflamed splashes
framed and hanging
in the Volunteer Park Museum.


3.
By day I loved
the farmhouse on the hill
the dust haze the pickup raised
plying the dirt roads
the orchard trees in even
rows down the slopes
and out in all directions
the sigh of apricots,
Santa Rosa plums, Bing
and Queen Anne cherries
ripening in the dry heat
the long-short snick snick
of the sprinklers' jerky rotation
hum and hiss of a low-flying
spray plane

In over-the-knees rubber boots
my cousin and I stomped
the uneven ground    careful
of cow pies and Canada thistles
plucked alfalfa shoots

to stick between our teeth
swaggered like cowboys
to the edge of the irrigation ditch
and stripped to swim in its muddied water
giddy on the danger of going too near
the whirlpool pull
of the main pipe's undertow

But after dark
in the attic room
in that house on the hill
he always fell asleep first,
leaving me alone
with the sounds of the night—

a coyote's cry,
the twist and scrape of tumbleweed
like a wind-tossed tangle of bones
over clay-dry earth,
a jackrabbit caught
in a jeep's headlight—

and everywhere the eerie
whine of the wind aprowl
in the Yakima night—
atonal, weedy, persistent


4.                    (Going Home Again)
The grass in the back reached all the way
to the victory garden, and the house,
freshly stuccoed, was aswirl afternoons
in chiaroscuro from the tall maple

now vanished, a verandah where it stood.  Thus
abbreviated, the lawn on the bay side
slopes too abruptly down
onto the dock where high tide hides

the barnacled rocks I scuttled over in bare feet,
the starfish I set out to stiffen and die
in the sun, the lop-clawed fiddle crab
I was frightened by.  But when

the present owner opens
the back door onto a kitchen, unclean
and cluttered as never in my mother's day,
I find the breakfast nook still in its place,
and just beyond—the dining room,
contracted, though otherwise the same—
the scene of that Sunday dinner I
choked on, our pet rabbit
dished up as chicken
because we were at war.


5.
We inherited Old Mike
with the Phinney Bay place,
entailed to the land
or it to him. I was too young
to understand and no one's left to say.
But I learned early to walk
wary of Old Mike's cane,
having lost one cat
to its spiteful swing
though the grownups all maintained
she died a natural death.
Yet somebody stuffed a long-haired calico
into a stone-weighted gunny sack
and dumped him, one summer afternoon,
into the river near our cabin.
Hauled out in time by Uncle Al,
he lived out his days, curled
under Miss Otis's grand, listening
to children's scales and arpeggios,
while Old Mike performed odd jobs

around the house and yard,
dragging his stiff leg,
my mother complaining of his smell.
He invited me once
into his cramped, linoleumed shack,
where he never had cronies in for cards.
I never thought to ask where he went
for Christmas or Thanksgiving.
And when we sold and moved away,
Old Mike, still alive,
was thrown into the bargain.

Now I'm the age he was then
I think of him and his entailment:
not the cushy berth of a piano teacher's cat,
but several steps up from a strip
of corrugated cardboard on the corner,
cane resting by a cup for coins.


6.
The hooded figure of Uncle Bob
slips into my sleep,
presses a picture into my hand
of him and me, drenched, towel-swaddled,
standing together against a pine-panelled wall.

And yet I never saw him
swimming or caught in the rain. Dapper

dresser, golf-playing butcher,
he gave us the choicest cuts.
No one could crack and clean
a fresh-cooked Dungeness
finer. I keep his stories—

about the elderly customer's Christmas turkey,
slaughtered early and hung to age
until cavity and carcass were basted

with a slime of green-white mould
Bob, the apprentice, had to sponge away;

about the way my father, the eldest son,
browbeat and bullied his brother—
haul this, drive me there, fetch me that—
though Bob, in girth and height,
soon outgrew him, a Lab
to his fox terrier;

about the first time Bob glimpsed
my Mom-to-be—standing
by a conveyor belt, hands flying
like Charlie Chaplin's
as she picked up one tumbling fruit after another
to discard or tissue-wrap and box—
the fastest apple packer in Yakima.

Sunday breakfasts at the cabin:
*Dearly beloved, gather round and put*
*your hand on the radio, feel the power*
*of the Lord.* Mom's face
faltering between grin and frown,
memories stirred of Dirty Thirties'
revivalists, how they'd descend
on Enumclaw, Wenatchee, Chelan,
Cle Elum, Wapato, Toppenish, Spokane,
pitch their tents, and rob the dirt-poor
farmers blind.  I squint

at rain-soaked Uncle Bob and me:
I'm bathing in his smile.

The November night my cousin called
to say her father had died, rain lashed
the windshield of Uncle Bob's car,
the two of us, lost, somewhere outside Seattle,
peering into the dark.

7.
I know the rocks from here to the bend
like the contours of my body.
Hugging the river bed, they hump and
jut, and from August to late September stretch out
and bask lizard-like in the sun.

The smoke from the stone fireplace
enters my pores, the strands
of my hair. Pebbles picked up from the bank
I finger like worry beads,
and line up, tiny talismans, along the window sill.

Time was I would slip with a friend
under the icy water, glide downstream,
eyes open for periwinkle, pepper
and salt of their twig-like casings,
perfect camouflage. And later,

falling asleep I'd imagine a saucer
hollowed out of the river bed,
an inverse pillow to lay my face upon,
listen to the incessant conversation of river
with rock, until consciousness sank into stone.


8.
Squalls, fog, days of drizzle,
rarely a sky unstained by cloud.
Modest, set-back-from-the-road
white frame houses rising
a story or two above mowed
but not manicured lawns,
the occasional flowerpot of petunias
or hanging basket of impatiens:
a neighbourhood of windows
like darkened lenses, closed
doors unlocked, cracked
and buckling sidewalks.

*Hell bent for a lecture,*
her mother's verdict. And hell bent
she was, back then, to escape
the sweet but choking air. The resplendent,
snow-domed mountains that fenced her—
The sailboats lazily cruising the lake,
affronts to ambition, to purpose—

Now when she returns, the beauty of the place
astonishes her.
Yet she still hears in her relatives'
*This is God's country, after all,*
an implicit *How could you have left!?*
and reads in appraising eyes
the old "hell bent" judgment
that sent her packing sends her ransacking
her purse to check for the ticket out.

9.                          (The Garden on Ruffner Road)
I can see only parts of it now,
—stone steps leading down
into a rendition of Eden. Glimpsed first
at its best—in April: azaleas
in shades of salmon and fuchsia,
the brasher-than-crayola pink
of a Japanese cherry,
a blossoming hybrid that crossed
apricot with peach.
No one took as an omen
the fissure the '52 quake
rent in the fishpond's foundation,
everyone grateful for such
minor damage.  And the shadow,
black as a Jesuit soutane,
crept in so imperceptibly,
stealing across the lawn, tainting
the tips of mother's spiky dahlias,
slithering up the trunk and dimming

the dogwood's five-pointed stars.  I marvel
at the sang-froid of the I
I was then, sitting with my back propped
against the rockery wall, studying
Milton's *Paradise Lost*
and carrying on as though
ours would last forever.

# The Thirteenth Element

The honourable Sir Robert Boyle was obsessed
with all that glows—carbuncles, rotting fish—
but especially phosphorous, a substance
the alchemist Brandt of Hamburg had discovered,
but kept a secret. Suspecting the source
in the urine's "golden stream," Boyle
nightly dispatched his laboratory lackeys
to collect the chamber pots of Pall Mall.
Boiling the piss and then heating the residue
until red hot, he finally produced
not only the stench of sulphur and onions
but his famous recipe, posthumously released.
                              In thus capturing
the elixir of life, his achievement ranks
with Frankenstein's, for the thirteenth element,
essential to the ecosystems of the earth,
has an affinity to fire, a talent for combustion,
that may have shone first in the innocent flare
of a match—but a century later stunned
the residents of Hamburg, Braunschweig, Dresden
with eels of incendiary light
writhing out of the sky.
                              A child at that time
I came across the innocuous
kin of Boyle's obsession
the summer camp night two of us rowed
over the unfathomable dark of Hood Canal
into a backwater and glimpsed,
coy in the depths,
tiny bursts of luminescence swirling.

# *O*bligue Light

I should be able to figure out
this raw unease I'm left with
after our taking tea and viewing
the Rubens' from Russia.

I should be able to name what has caused
this constriction around my heart,
this queasiness wedged in my belly.
As the day winds down the light

takes on an indirectness and the wind
blows March-like though we're halfway
to June.  Do feelings belong more
to the body than to the mind?

Riding the streetcar home, I open
Farías. He says Heidegger stayed
gung-ho National Socialist
to the end, roping his concept

of transcendental Being
to the cause, to cries for combat, *Kampf,*
Aryan purity; poetry's purpose
to bring *das* Germanic *Volk*

into sync with its true essence,
its historic role to save
the decadent West.  The streetcar,
turning short, drops me at Lansdowne,

a no-man's land before the Dundas bridge
over the railway tracks leading
out of town.  I walk a block
to the College Car but it's replaced

by buses and they're running
late. The sun's oblique light
brightens but doesn't warm.  Maybe
it was his snapping *Someday*

*I should draw you a family tree*
after I'd asked, to show interest,
how he came to have a cousin
to visit in Zeitz. Perhaps I share

Heidigger's belief in *Blut*
*und Boden*?  Standing here
on this wind-bruised corner,
the sore somewhere at my centre

harder to heal than the blister
on my right hand's palm, I'm
like a rattled leaf that lacks
understanding of the wind's purpose.

*T*he Grand Narrative

> has lost its credibility, regardless of what mode of unification
> it uses, regardless of whether it is a speculative narrative or a narrative
> of emancipation.
>
> *Jean-François Lyotard*


was always about a phoenix,
re-fleshed, fledged, and flapping up
out of the pyre's ashes. A rood

on Calvary and the stone rolled away
from an empty tomb. An owl,
nocturnal, Athenian, taking wing

as day darkens to dusk.
A bedtime story about a crystal
slipper and the right fit.

It could be most elaborately
embroidered, bars and bright stars stitched
into the fabric. Liberty, agility, fraternity

bannered, carried mud-spattered and torn
over the heads of the throng: *das Volk*,
*le peuple*. "Being-in-the-world" alchemized

not into nothingness but into something
riven with possibility, transcendent:
the Victorian paterfamilias, a Master

Race. Blood, thicker than water,
spills identically, the strutting protagonists
buddy-buddy with the gibbet, the *KZ*.

Tumbrel. Gulag. Everything in the name of
you name it, an answer to the bedevilling question
on your final exam: *der Tod ist ein Meister*

*aus Deutschland*    and *Amerika*.
Remember the Alamo.  Bottom
of the ninth. Little House on the Prairie.

# The Scent of an Orange

1.
I saw it out the train window
on the way to Basel and, coming back,
saw it again—a ladder
propped against the unpruned branches of a tree,
plum or maybe pear, head lost
in the leaves, feet planted in the grass
of an unkempt orchard, wooden shafts
weather-warped, rungs worn round
by calloused hands, mud-caked boots—poor

country cousin to the ladder painted
on the church wall in Wernigerode,
growing like a beanstalk up from the earth,
wafting down from the sky like Rapunzel's
golden hair—too fine to bear bodies
corpulent with desire,
only the coming and going of angels
guarding the few souls chosen
to ascend into sun-pierced clouds
and beyond (out of sleeping Jakob's sight)
the deadly peace of heaven.


2.
Last year there I wished
I were here, and now,
here, I don't really wish
to return to the barbed *Schwierigkeiten*
of my forgotten German
I so wanted to learn again.  Easier said
trips off the tongue
but there nothing was said easily. With every

*Satz* I stepped outside meanings onto a field
strung with trip wires. Stranded. Sixty and almost

silent, reduced to halting,
childlike speech;
to enter an early senility
and all for what?
I think, now that I can think again
in English—it was for love, a
neglected *Liebe*, and I hear *die Tauben*
cooing outside my window:
I'm seventeen, on legs fast as scissor blades,
dashing down the stairs
and out into cobbled streets,
that clangorous belled sky.


3.
On second thought
it was less for love
I returned than for
the scent of an orange
I peel and section for *Vati*,
the tile stove I hug for warmth
singeing my skirt.  Home from school
Traminer grapes from *Mutti*
by my bed, windows I push open
like doors.  At night listening
for the *plupp* of the cork,
Gisela and her fiancé. Birds
at dawn after a fancy dress ball,
I, Madame Butterfly,
dizzy from drink
and dancing polka with Jürgen.
Crisp crusted *Brötchen* for breakfast,
plates piled high with *Kartoffeln* midday.
I'd even welcome

*Meckerziegenschwester* Renate—
anything to be transported
back to then.


It's not there anymore: the apartment,
the cobbled *Hof.* No weekly *Kaffeeklatsch*
for Mutti; for Gisela, nothing but bed
and a mindless body hitched to tubes.
As for *Kronprinz* Jürgen, an inheritance
squandered, and Renate finding him in Munich,
in that rented, bottle-strewn room,
his head blown off.
Were his last thoughts
of *Vati's Kaufhaus*,
bought cheap from fleeing Jews,
or of Uschi, the Rhenish beauty?


4.                        (*Vati's* **Orange**)
The scent, yes,
but also the feel
of the nippled orb,
shy shine on its puckered skin:
my task, sitting at the left hand
of *Vati*, to strip off the peel,
lay bare (without tearing)
an inner flesh traversed
by whitish threads, trace
of segmentation. Then
to separate one section
from the next, running again
the risk of a tear leaking
sweet, sticky fluid
down my fingers. I was
seventeen and full
of desire
(he had me brush his hair)
to please *Vati*, fifty,
(wispy hair, soft bristled brush).

I, the chosen one,
preferred over *Mutti*, Gisela, Renate,
to perform *Vati*'s
after-dinner
*Apfelsine*,
the brush's caress:
these maiden rituals.


5.                              (The Pink Shoes)
Ten years after war's over
it's still post-war: *Ersatzkaffee*,
*Ersatzbutter*.  But no ersatz
for the woman strapped to a plough,
straining across the field.  Nor
for the buildings, however grotesque,
filling gaps in the broken rows
of gabled roofs, half-timbered houses.
Drab figures shuffle
over rubble-cleared ground, bursts
of colour *verboten*.  But in Cologne,

beyond the cathedral's skeletal shadow,
a pair of shoes in a shop window:
pink kid, with three-cornered heels
like the cocked hat of the song.  My *Mutti*
and *Vati*, in their chauffeured Mercedes,
they bought me, goodwill visitor
from the land of the victors,
those reparation, time-of-renewal,
reconciliation shoes.
            And they became
my prancing shoes, my skipping-
over-cobblestones-past-ruins shoes,
my Viennese-waltzing-with-Opa,
polka-dancing-with-Jürgen, once-
in-a-lifetime,
                never-to-be-duplicated,
almond-pink-blossom shoes.

6.

It's a short drive from Frankfurt to Lützelbach, to the *Altersheim* where Gisela lies, broomstick-thin arms outside the sheets, skin translucent as the plastic tubes feeding and relieving her. Uwe strokes her sleep-drugged cheek, no real hope of recognition, the eyes she opens not her own eyes. "I'm sorry I didn't come earlier to say goodbye, I tried, but I couldn't get away." Senseless to explain. My tears focus on some inner realm. Afterwards Aschaffenburg, a small exhibit in a church hall of Emil Nolde *Aquarellen*. Uwe didn't need to take me, it's out of the way, and not his cup of tea, a sort of art he might still think "*entartet*," denounced by the Nazis as diseased, but I don't ask, just pretend he's as interested as I. In a glass showcase in the centre of the room, a selection of Nolde's "*ungemalte Bilder*," painted when he was forbidden to paint, no larger than a hand. Feats of distillation, but no crossing over into absence, like Gisela. One's a portrait of a woman, eyes downcast, her face and neck yellow and green, mouth a smudge of red. I look up, catch Uwe gazing at it too, wonder what he sees.


7.

My eyes open on the bedroom curtain
haloed by sun seeping between fabric
and frame. A moon in eclipse looks like this,
the light of its countenance never fully obscured,
only veiled as though with a brocade mask
the colours of pumpkin and marzipan.

I remember how, during the war,
blackout shades were drawn
not to keep moonlight out
but our lamplight in
so the enemy couldn't detect
where uninhabited country left off
and towns and cities began.

V.J. Day '45 my brother and I
rowed the dinghy mid-bay

loaded with lids from our mother's saucepans
we beat like cymbals
to celebrate the raised curtain,
the light flooding in.

Bright-eyed American teenager in '55,
I told my German hosts the tale
of banging lids, till hushed
by the shadow that descended
like a curtain over every countenance:
the spectre of cities reduced to rubble,
eight-year-old Gisela running home,
*Weberstraße* razed,
front door buried under burning ruins.


8.
*Ruthchen*, they call, and I wake.
A floor below, the clink and rattle
of preparations for *Kaffeetrinken*.
May sun dapples the terrace.
Under the *Marquise,* a table set
with blue and white patterned china
and linen napkins in silver rings.
Carillons of larkspur chime violet-blue
and blackbirds and chickadees chirp
from *Hecke* to hedge.  The coffee pot
is brought, the *Kuchen* cut into slices
and lifted onto plates.  We sip
and talk inconsequentially.
                              Thus memory
colludes with longing,
for no one calls my name, and I wake
not there, but here, Gisela
as good as nowhere, and Uwe
no longer the Uwe I knew.

9.                    (Die Wacht am Rhein)
Massed above my train
white sky-borne fleece rises
in the shape of that first amphibian
climbing out of the muck,
anvil head extended on bull neck,
appendages in a *zick, zack*
of grasping struggle,
body's *Schwung* a giant
S like one of the serpentine curves
the Rhine scores between Koblenz
and Mainz.

Why do I read the sky
over this country and not my own
like a Rorschach of savage *Kampf*?
Castles of mediaeval warring knights
crown the sheer and jagged cliffs,
HOTEL emblazoned on their once
unassailable fortifications. Massive
*Germania* towers above Rüdesheim.
One arm slices the air with her sceptre,
the other holds aloft a victor's orb
to Prussia, unifier of Germany,
now swept away, mostly, into Poland.

Gunnels barely skimming the water,
coal-laden barges chug up river,
both coal and water sun-spangled
like the *Gipfel* of the *Loreley* crags
made famous by the German Jew
Heinrich Heine.
        *Ich weiß nicht, was soll es bedeuten,*
        *Daß ich so traurig bin...*
a melancholy poem so beloved by Germans
it could not be rooted out.

Glimpses, beneath the present,
flow across my train window.
Near the end of the line islands appear
as overhead the monstrous cloud dissolves,
sloughs off its reptilian contours, and calm
settles dream-like on the widening river.

# *P*ost-war Photo

Just try to expunge
that Vogue photographer's
photo from your mind,
the one she snapped of herself
posed naked (or half-naked,
one sees only her upper body)
in Hitler's bathtub.

Did she picture him
cleaning his teeth, clipping his *Zehennägel*,
washing his face?  Imagine
him unclothed,
stepping into a *Badewanne*
to scrub his back,
his legs—

You try to picture her,
unbuckling and kicking off her combat boots,
soiled from shoots at Dachau, Buchenwald,
stripping off her baggy wool fatigues,
slipping herself in between the walls
of curved white porcelain.

Was she, American *naïf,*
seeking the *frisson*
of a brush with power?
Or was her photo a way
of thumbing her nose at him,
whose orders stripped others
naked?

She grimly faces the camera, eyes turned
upward and to the side. Behind her head
a bar of soap lies in a dish.
The *Waschlappen* in her right hand, crossed
to her left shoulder, wiping what away?

# *C*eremony

            I want entry
into a world of more ceremony,
as in the story Yuk Lin told
about a make of clay pot, very rare,
very expensive: if only used to brew
a single variety of tea, say white peonie,
after many years the pot will prepare,
without leaves, without blossoms,
the finest imaginable infusion of that tea
                    from memory.

# *T*he Gift

1.
Brought up on the idea
it's better to give,
the young girl has given
her mother a gift she's
not happy to receive,
openly scorns as ugly,
cheap: a sewing kit the girl
loved for its cylindrical shape
like a box for a very tall hat.
Its material only cardboard,
but encased in quilted turquoise plastic
with a handle of gold braided cord
and a shelf inside that lifted out,
a round, shallow tray divided
into wedge-shaped pieces like a pie.

Forty years later the daughter
returns to open cupboards, drawers,
and sort through her mother's
closets full of dresses, shoes, coats,
shelves piled with sweaters, hats
and yards of fabric already chalk
marked and cut along the lines
of rustling paper patterns pinned
to the cloth. And there, in a corner:
the sewing kit crammed
with a jumble of thread-wound
bobbins and spools, mending yarn,
buttons, needles, pins,
and pinking shears—a crack
in the turquoise plastic,
the gold braid handle frayed.

2.
Beyond the dishwasher's drone
a silence grows, a silence of the sort
parents fear when their kids
are somewhere near, but out of sight.
                              I find her
on her knees in the unlit kitchen, frantic
to hold back, with bare hands and towel,
a spew of suds gushing
from the seams of the machine.  Why

couldn't I have simply knelt and joined
in the act of mopping up, but no,
screaming *Mother! What have you done?*
I turned up the heat under a pot
already seething. As though struck
she raced, shrieking, from the room
to return wielding a broom I try
to wrench from her hands, she resists,
her strength super-human, swiping
at the mounting foam, driving it
in jagged streams across the tiles.


3.
My always impeccably groomed mother
sits bare assed,
tied to a potty chair on wheels,
scant apron across her lap:
private parts
no longer private here.
Age has strip-mined her mind,
stretched the skin on her head skull-tight,
shrivelled her body so thin the wedding ring
she wore for more than fifty years
slipped off her finger.

Front tooth chipped,
she gives me a hag's leer,
grabs my hand, begs
*take me out of this place*
*anywhere*

*home.*  But home has suffered a diaspora:
the objects that defined her life
dispersed to nephew, niece, neighbour—
muffin tins, piano, embroidered
pillow cases—
a household hit by hurricane.

I spoon ice cream
between her gums;
she confides in me,
a stranger, how hard
it is to mother a daughter
who expects too much,
demands that she
be perfect.

Leaning in I whisper
*But you were:*

*it was so easy*
*to leave in your hands the iron*
*you snatched from mine,*
*to leave to you the needles and pins,*
*scrub mop, the crack in the lid*
*of the flowered tea pot.*

4.
My mother, alive again, black hair
unstreaked with grey, face no more lined
than mine at forty, strides into my life,
Katherine Hepburn playing Amelia Earhart,
takes command. I go along
for the ride—racing along a canyon
blasted through the middle of a sky-scraping city.
Once the car hangs so
steeply over the decline, to drive on means
to leave the road, sail off
into clear space, a dare my
devil-may-care mother
takes
          and lands us, without a jolt, upright.
In the dream she's younger than I am now,
and the landscape lacks all correspondence
to our home town—though I do recall that time,
before there was a name for her addled state,
she drove me across the city on the I-5,
taking hair-raising chances as she switched lanes
and cut in front of other cars with aplomb—
I, an unwilling passenger, caught
between wish and fear, thinking that she,
a church-going woman in thrall all her life
to the strictest of rules, had cast them off
toward the end because
that end was near.


5.
I know, when she visits at night, who she is.
                    Take last night:
swigging champagne, knocking it back
straight out of the bottle
as she slammed down winning hands
and laughed it up with Auntie Viv and Cousin Chris
under the slanted ceiling of my teenage bedroom.
I stood off in a corner pulling piles

of folded clothes from a closet,
holding myself back, thinking—
how strange to see my teetotal mother
let go.
                    She always ran
a tight ship, pitching housework goals so high
I failed to learn to cook or can; my only task,
besides the dinner dishes, to hang out the wash:
she trusted me with that; and how I loved
to hold up each dripping piece, press
the notch of the wooden peg down tight
over the line, and in twilight
gather the sheets, pants, shirts,
towels, now dry, and cart them in,
blended with the scent of grass.
                    We never
shared a drink, or a laugh, that I remember.
Clothes were our bond, even though she thought
I ironed wrinkles in instead of out
and never taught me how to sew: shopping
we met on common ground. Sporting hats, gloves,
heels, we'd go downtown, to Frederic's or the Bon,
visit the tea room, take a look around—
                              she,
leaning back in the fitting room chair,
sizes up the skirt and sweater I put on.

# *F*alling

In dreams she begins to fall,
sprawling on her back—
Nell Severance in *Swamp Angel*—
a gigantic, wizened turtle overturned,
unable to rise, to right herself.

During the day she steps out
her door onto sidewalk
like a novice skater onto ice,
clutching her walking stick,
a heavy flag cleaving to its staff.

Fall is loss. She thinks of falling
asleep, of autumn's penance, Lucifer's
legion of fallen angels, Adam and Eve's
expulsion, her own lost balance,
dignity. But, oh, to fall

in love again, to lose oneself in another,
the way the woman there
strokes the man's shoulder,
walks off with him into the yellowing larch.

*D*reaming *of this place*

takes me back to the Red Robin Tavern
and that long swoon of a summer
I spent over the blue moon in love
with the hirsute bartender from Birmingham,
the way he slapped down pitchers of watery beer
and later propped me upright down the sloping
path to his houseboat on Union Bay
to roll in a never-made bed and feel
the waves swell and abate, swell and abate.

The piss yellow of the light and the beer's
the same but this dive is hazy with smoke,
I barely make out the guy tending bar, my eyes,
thirty years older, fasten on a closer,
younger man in rumpled shirt—
a regular, hunched over his drink,
he drags on his cigarette, interest unlit.
He drags on his cigarette, interest unlit—

*This Messy In-Between*

The hangers-on still
glow golden as yellow velvet dresses
swinging from a pole-rack.

Spilling singly, they float past his window
the way clothes shed by a sky-diving stripper
might waft, trembling, to the ground.

But he's grown impatient
with the linden's slow disrobing,
this messy in-between,

and hankers instead
for the Dürer-sharp lines
of naked branches
raking grey sky.

# *C*oncrete Image

Ready, by the look of them,
for putting out to pasture:
four sawhorses barricade
fresh sections of sidewalk
between Bedford and Bloor,
each stamped MAPLE CRETE INC. 1999
like a hallmark on the handle of a silver fork.
How I wanted as a child to leave my mark
on fresh pavement's shiny, wet surface.
But then I was too vigilantly watched. Now,
no one notices as I crouch, slip
my hand under one horse's slatted shanks
and slap five fingers and the heel of one palm
into the ridged, concrete dough,
then scramble up and walk fast,
hand held away from my side,
down the street and around the corner
into the Ladies at Greg's Ice Cream.

# *K*ansas Largesse

Mornings the farm house pings with light
as though klieg-lit—no, not
that false brightness, flashy as a
rhinestone brooch, but pure, buoyant,
ebullient. Even.  Breathing in
I float up to the ceiling's peak,
waft around like a tipsy dust mote,
then drift out a window to sail

over blond-stubbled, mud-black fields
past the hedgerow of osage orange and cedar
where yesterday Frank's hunting dogs
flushed out four quail.  A soaring spiral
around the silo on the eastern horizon
before circling back over gravel roads

to re-enter the sun-glazed, oven-warm kitchen
where I spatula, from baking sheet onto cooling rack,
cookies, round and brown as buttons on a greatcoat,
and offer them in a new, dough-spattered expansiveness.

# *B*etween Iola and Moran

Headed for the family farm
between Iola and Moran,
we pass through La Harpe and Gas,
formerly Gas City but the water tower
now reads only Gas. We drive by the caved-in
Swan Johnson place, the hollow stare of its windows,
see a Cooper's Hawk high in an Oak,
coppery brown leaves aquiver. Like hands
flailing above water, the fallen ones
sticking out of the snow flutter
in the December wind. Black orbs
hang in the Osage Orange, Christmas
ornaments clinging to a charred tree.
We swerve to keep from turning
a rufous fox into road kill. Last year, Mark says,
La Harpe voted against a community centre
but for the sale of liquor
by the drink. Meadowlarks swarm
the shoulder of the road, foraging grit.
Gravel is necessary for the craw. Once brome,
here, was called rich man's grass.

# Summer Jobs

Bees graze the hydrangea
like tiny speeded-up cows
scrambling head down over clustered
mounds of little petals, sometimes losing
balance, the branch stem bobbing but
not so jerkily as the pickerelweed nudged
by goldfish in some game of tag they play,
taking a break from their endless circling
and gliding.  They leap through
the fountain's jets or nibble
at the water hyacinth roots. Indefatigable
in their coasting rounds, these submerged
dirigibles patrol the pond, orange,
poised, sure they can outdart,
with a languid flick of translucent
fins and tail, raccoon
or cat or black-feathered crow.

# *A*ngels in the Snow

*We're overdosing on aesthetic pleasure,*
you said from under your black toque,
and it was true—as we walked
through the deep, limestone gorge
along the edge of the snow-laced creek
into a lattice of trees, the mesh
of their snow-traced branches
like a black-on-white paisley of angel wings
growing indistinct in the thickening snow.
Its fall the hush of angel dust.  And us,
surprised witnesses to the coalescing
of the beautiful and true.  Who
but the angelic can sustain such rapture?
We endured only small, isolated
epiphanies, one after one
until we flung our bodies
down into the deepening whiteness,
semaphoring our awe.

*Below "Imponderable," a Yellowed Iris*

1.                    **(The Abbey in Fall)**
Out over rows of cornstalks stirring
like skins poled to dry in the wind, the bell
tower tolls the hours.  Between the cornfields,
sun-flowers stand in defeated lines, heads hanging,
or headless, their dead-green leaves curled.
A mound of poppies slumps, the orange bloom bruised
but still vivid after the frost.  Raspberry canes,
tattered, fruitless.  And under cloud-creased sky,
concentrically hedged by blue spruce and cedar: the Brothers'
graveyard—white granite headstones in ordered
rows to the rear of their founder's monument.


2.
Nothing to say, no one to say it to, I go
to take a picture of the blighted sunflowers,
but they're gone—torn out, ploughed under,
furrowed soil where they stood.  Further along,
beyond the hen house, a young pig's thin corpse
curls foetally around an old tire. A barn cat
cleans itself in the sun less than a foot away.

Looped over the paling of a silvered rail fence
a coil of rusty barbed wire.  A magpie's shadow
passes over the yellow prairie grass.

In a gulley at the side of the road a scattering
of small, black mounds like land mines.
A pick-up truck rattles by: I wave
and the driver waves back.
I still have gestures.

3.
From across fields of winter rye,
a train whistles—the prairie loon.
I withdraw into the microcosm of my room,
                              wait
for the space heater to whir into warmth,
the radiator pinging like a plucked harp.
The blue towel hanging from a ceiling hook
—the Virgin Mary ascending. Overhead
the floorboards creak as Barbara
walks in paradise.


4.
Breaking the still of the library, I follow
a young, black-robed Brother down spiral stairs,
metal clanging like Chinese gongs,
through laden grey stacks to the back
where old dictionaries, retired from Reference,
sit cover to cover in shabby disuse. I pull
*Weatherly's Imperial English* from the shelf, turn
to "E" for "enclaustered" and find, pressed between the pages,
beneath "earthwork" and "earth-worm," as thin as the wings
of a butterfly, bleached of all but a trace of purple,
a morning-glory bloom. And at the letter "I,"
by "implore," a three-leaf clover, its green holding;
below "imponderable," a yellowed iris
with a flattened calyx. Checking out the tome, my hand
brushes the Brother's as he reglues
the date-due sheet on the marbled inner cover.
Later, at my desk, I riffle the pages back and forth,
back and forth, till I'm rewarded with a Prairie crocus
between "brew" and "bric-a-brac," two red,
serrated leaves under "tabernacle," and forget
what I went in search of.

5.
Brother Basil leads us out a scullery door,
early Christians entering the catacombs,
down a corridor tunnelled deep beneath the Abbey
into an underground chamber braced with shelves
on every wall—a library of preserves
newly massed after the fall harvest, stocked
in the past by nuns for love of God, now
by women from the town for pay, but either way
with arms up to their elbows in brilliant juices,
then standing the jars of stewed tomatoes,
chokecherry jelly, small white pears
on their heads to check the sealers
for telltale bubbles before righting them
to store in row stacked on row, glowing
dimly from within like a saint's countenance.


6.                    (Leo)
Once visited by Jesus and John the Baptist,
he's still called The Hermit ten years
after he moved from monastery into Muenster
to a sunshine yellow house
within a rainbow-painted paling fence,
a sightseeing attraction on the main drag into town.
A gallery of Delft plates from his Holland home,
crucifixes, plaster Virgins, a bleeding heart,
and every centimetre of wall from hall to bedroom, porch
to kitchen, hung with visions: sunflowers
shining from outer space, a fruit-studded pudding
auraed in orange, a Dutch windmill afloat
in blue prairie sky. And fertility,
a three-foot ovum impregnated
with parti-coloured chains of DNA
and a burst of red, egg-shaped tulips—
a complex but maculate conception.

7.                       (Saying Goodbye to the Abbey)
Brown leaves under a scrim of frost.  Groaning
an auger sucks up wheat from a truck,
spirals it into a silo. Elevators already full
though no one's been able to combine all week
because of the wet.  Deep furrows
score the earth at the base of the oaks.
On the crest of the path to Muenster,
a stand of sapling aspen, stripped bare:
silver broom straws scraping grey sky.
A chill wind rasps the last of the cornstalks.
Reentering St. Scholastica I hear
everyone packing, Pam
crying in an upstairs room, Marlene,
next door, humming ballad shards.


8.                            (Back Home)
Sky hidden by the grey anatomy
of branches, antennae, hydro lines.
I shrink under the press of houses
too close, the weight of buildings
taller than what seems safe, pavement
ungiving beneath my feet.  Then

a reprieve: sun, and a rainbow
high-jumps over billboards.
A grizzled man looks up
from his blighted garden
to hand me a clutch of dahlias,
their quilled and tufted petals
unstricken by the recent freeze.

9.                          (Return)
Sloughs brim with the crackle of frogs
we never heard last fall,
and ducks we rarely saw in the woods
flap up this spring, squawking,
from every jack pine and cedar.
There's only the skeleton
of oaks over the cemetery road,
arched umbrella ribs stripped
bare.  I follow the path
to the cabin, peer
through a window's film
at the table covered now
with oilcloth, no
clutter of pens, pencils, poems,
the hut's air as still
as the sky.  Sun
warms my skin and the wind
is your breath on the back of my neck,
but I know if I turn round, you
can't be there.  The chickadees
have returned, though—look, one lands,
picks at seeds I hold in my outstretched palm.


10.                          (Pender Island, April 16, 1997)
Shadowed by crow harassing hawk,
we begin our ascent of Mount Norman,
eased into a new intimacy
after last night's lashing rain, wine,
talk of dark eros.  Our trail,
unlike Petrarch's up Mount Ventoux,
grants no fork to a gentler route,
only steepens stonily. *What is that?*

*and that*? I ask and you name
*salal, arbutus, flowering currant.* Warmed
by the heat of the mid-morning sun
we shed our hats, anoraks—trade
tales of former lives, loves.
At the summit, high
in the Giotto blue
eagles coast air currents,
circling, pairing

# *S*onnenizio on a Line from Rilke


*Ein Hauch um Nichts. Ein Wehn im Gott. Ein Wind.*
A breath about nothing. A gust inside the god. A wind.
So Orpheus sang with the sweet wildness of a wind rose
that grows not in window-boxes among petunias and geraniums
but in scattered clusters on the forest floor, white and wind-blown,
his voice responsive as a wind-chime to every stirring of breeze,
a wind instrument supplely tempered, its sound swift
to soar, then glide, borne aloft on currents of wind.
He was to poetry and song what the windhover is to flight,
until on that winding ascent from Pluto's netherworld
he turned, winded, and looked back, wanting but a moment's
inspiration, and in whirling knocked the wind
out of Eurydice, his love, crumpled like a wind-sock
after the wind drops, doomed to Hades and songlessness.

# Nachlaß

That morning I longed to leave, but the lake
lay calm as an empty mall, pink
as putti's cheeks. From
an encircling crack of light
between the horizon and cloud's thick curtain
came sunrise's *Nachlaß*.
I yearned to give alms
to all who caulk boats against leaks
and rake leaves from
under trees. This was no callow ache
a casual gesture might still.
I settled for filling an urn
with unculled longings.

# *A*fter a Poem by Paul Celan

Morning mirrors night.  I watch
from across the table your eyes
weeping blue for a love
brewed by another.  Waves
of emptiness pass between us.
Once we lay together
faster than sea laps up sky.
I lay myself down now an empty
autumn thing.  Oh to drink
sea-deep of what we had
then when we had
summer and ourselves.

# *L*ay the Bitter to Rest

1.
Falling through moss-hung trees
across salmonberry and wild geranium,
onto crumbling cedar and fir-needled paths,
this angled splash of sunlight
washing the green of rain forest
shines with the innocence of a time
before that time you manoeuvred the sloop
alongside yachts and cabin cruisers,
a wake tail-finning out behind,
past schooners named Paragon,
Daybreak, Sweet Surrender,
into an out-of-the-way island harbour—
tied first the stern, then the bow line to the dock,
and lifted me out onto dry land.


2.
We coddled the two hawthorns
for six years,
costly feed,
frequent sprayings,
but susceptivity
to insects, mould,
and every disease known to tree
left us little
choice in the end.

We lop off the limbs
almost leafless
(though only August),
saw the trunks
into cordwood, take
shovel and axe
to the thick, deeply spread

roots, digging,
whacking, yanking,
their hold on life
at odds with the trees'
sickly foliage.

We choose a ginkgo
to fill the hole
in the back garden.
An ancient tree,
the nursery attendant says,
and hardy.  For proof
she tells the story
of a ginkgo uprooted
and left exposed
all one winter.
Planted in the spring
it revived and throve.
Ours, with its fluttering
lemon-green leaves,
each like a banner
slit at one end,
seems frail.

Pulled from the truck,
a branch breaks off.
We attempt a re-grafting,
taping it tightly back
at the node where it hangs
by a strip of bark,
hoping sap will still run
beneath the rind.


3.
I had a husband once,
head like Einstein's on a
scarecrow body—scraggly beard,

pigeon breast,
at parties he'd perch
(well, hunker, really)
on chair or stool,
not utter a word
until everyone else had spoken,
then, taking out his pipe,
tamping down tobacco in the bowl,
he'd speak
and everyone would listen
for the momentous whatever he had to say,
something worth having waited to hear.
A case of the philosopher's beard.

I had a husband once,
we lived on Monkstown Road
in a rambling, Hitchcockian house
where we threw soirées, invited
everyone we knew
for home brew and Screech
and he flirted with other women
while I flirted with other men
and the pine floor bounced like a trampoline
and the octopus furnace belched and wheezed
and we stomped and swirled our way to sunrise
and then fell upstairs into solitary beds,
the door closing behind the last to leave.

I had a husband once
in rumpled khaki fatigues,
a lucky strike behind one ear,
who courted me with Yeats,
read by moonlight under the columns,
and knew, I thought, everything
about Bergman, Felini, Renoir,
phlogiston and Newton and Freud,
about Schinkel, Baron Haussmann and Christopher Wren,
Lawrence and Miller and Joyce,

but not about Lessing or Levertov, Woolf or Plath,
or Hannah Arendt and Melanie Klein,
or Wollstonecraft, Rich and Astell,
so not about everything, as I'd
let myself believe.

I had a husband once,
but I misled him
and he misled me
and we mislaid each other.


4.
At the end there were only
icy roads, fear,
and every night your standing the tavern crowd
to round after round of drinks
from our joint account,

and my waking to silence
stalking the rooms of that old house
now never to be renovated
beyond the half-assed job we did
on the ground floor.

What would you take
if you had to flee a burning house?
I've kept more old footage
from ours on Monkstown Road
than I might have realized
or let on
even a year ago:

in the grainy distance of one eroding frame
I see us, heads together,
running across a vacant lot
asway in wild yarrow and cratered

with puddles we jump in unison,
our hands
clasped for the moment
on the stem of a single
umbrella


5.
*Very Euro*, the clerk says of the black
leather shoes I buy the morning after
I dream of a cow's slaughter:

> past her prime,
> laid out on the counter, her coat
> shaggy as a mountain
> goat's, with a look

I can't shake though I plunge
into the maze of the mall, lose myself
in the jostle of shoppers out,
like me, for post-Christmas sales, pause
before the knocked down dresses in a shopwindow,
see my

> lover and his other
> woman about to wield the knife:
> *Don't worry*, they murmur. *We'll
> plunge her into heated water;
> she'll feel no pain.* But,

> while my head is turned, they
> drag the cow up a flight
> of stairs so steep and narrow I can't
> reach the landing at the top, its door
> bolted

> yet see-through and I glimpse,
> peering back through the glass, her
> wild, fear-flooded eyes.

6.                **(Asphodel)**
Careless, his throwing that party,
mid-summer, front door wide open
for her to stray through.
She who had known, like the Last Emperor,
only homage and enclosure.

For years after the divorce
it was not his ghost but hers
I spotted on front porches,
pursued down alleys,
calling her name—haunted
by the thought of what happened
to Asphodel that shadowless night,
as she made her slow
descent down unlit steps
and vanished into the dark.

On summer nights that descend
tentative and troubled,
I still grieve for her:
aloof except toward me,
her almond-shaped, amber eyes
      gleaming out of a sleek black lostness.


7.
Lay the bitter
            to rest. Let the you
I shared a past with become
a stranger who grew old among
others.
           Think of fresh oranges,
sliced into sixths and eaten
with fingers, teeth pulling away
*saftig* flesh from the peel's white
pulp, and you sucking
bits of meat from a boiled lobster's

thinnest leg.  I have no bone to pick
                    with the landscape—
the Narrows, the tumble of pastel
clapboard down the Battery's cliff,
the sharp climb from Water Street
up Prescott Hill to Rawlin's
Cross, the rise above Quidi
Vidi where, the morning after
a freezing rain, grass stalks tinkled
like a chandelier's crystal drops
swaying in the draft, a door closing.


                              Ether,
your eighteenth-century science believed,
fills all empty space.  Now
you're gone, I could return except
around every corner a mirage:
our first time hearing Haydn's
"Seven Last Words of Christ," seeing
Murnau's *The Last Laugh*, Renoir's
*La Grand Illusion*, our dismay
that anyone could offhandedly dismiss
von Strohheim's white gloves. Home

for your birthday that July,
you handed around glasses of wine,
mine last, a foretaste
of togetherness gone sour,
                         a shared study
split, the partners-desk buried
under stacks of books and, torn

from covers, sheet upon sheet
of letters from lovers, ex, current,
unfolded and smoothed out to lie
face up.
              Dealing five-card stud
on penny-ante poker nights,

you liked to affect a movie gambler's mien,
announcing before the final round:
last card down and dirty.


8.                         (Revision)
If I could go back to the beginning,
but where? To when he squats
on the bed in a shadowed room,
arms hugging knees to chest,
body rocking? He says he is in pain,
the pain of one-sided love
and I'm the cause as though I chose
to make him suffer. Years later he claims
I laughed cruelly. But I remember feeling
awe, indebtedness. And later

entitlement to his love, seizing it
as my ticket out. If I could go back
to the beginning, but years have passed.
And the stream follows a different course
or the ferns and alders have grown thicker,
more tangled. Searching, I circle
the periphery of where Christmas Creek
sluices toward the Snoqualmie, where I
laid myself out in shallow, fern-
and alder-shadowed water and pulled
him down onto me, our bodies jamming
the creek's flow.

I've led him to an innocent place,
a childhood place I stain with a scene
lifted from the silver screen or some
trashy novel, my body feigning
passion for my mind's sake. Should I trace
the source of the stream, the decay
at the heart of our coupling, to this
compound lie: the one I told my body,
the one my body told his—

light diffused through alder and fern,
brook's susurrus drowning any gasp
or moan he might have uttered, creek bed
hard and cold under my back,
swift indifferent rifts magnifying,
distorting the slippery, mottled rocks?

## Crossing the Steppes of Outer Mongolia

To make the space our own,
we shove the ping pong table
against a wall scarred black
by slammed racket balls.
Take our positions, feet
shoulder width apart,
balancing on the bubbling spring.
Daphne extends her arms laterally
and then back behind her spine,
an archival angel flexing pinions,
scooping air like water. Arms raised
to shoulder height, lowered,
palms down, we begin
the set.  I push out
with the back of my right hand,
palm of my left,
to grasp bird's tail, feathers
fluttering between fingers.
A slow pigeon-toed pivot
and Daphne rises up, silver-headed
stork, wings spread.
An untamedness enters us:
we carry tigers to mountains,
ward off monkeys,
strike other tigers left and right.
Crossing the Steppes of Outer Mongolia
we part the manes of wild horses,
watch a fair lady work shuttles.
A golden cock stands, unsteadily,
first on one leg, then the other.
Again and again our hands move
past our faces like gliding clouds.
Reaching a shore, we wade in,
push needles deep into sea bottom.
On an ebbing tide, we creep

low like a snake, bellying over sun-warmed
sand.  Rapt, we step up to catch
seven stars, retreat
to ride tiger. Then
in an explosion of drawn bows,
chopping fists, we deflect,
parry and punch.  The end nears,
we cross hands, exhale, bow,
and return to the room
of no clear purpose.

# The Hoodoos

You talk of Kashmir and the beginning
of mountains as we descend the slow slope
to walk along the winding Bow,
your words flowing as unevenly
as the river we watch
through openings in the trees.
Silver-grey, knurled roots,
scaly like chicken claws
crisscross the trail.
You easily master
the steep scramble
at the end, the loose rock
skittering from under boots
underscoring your hushed imperative: *Look!*
I turn, lean my back against a tree
that moves beneath my body,
and there, higher up, dun yellow
against an abyss of blue—sand,
shale, silt and stone
cemented and weather-eroded
into a giant hooded gnome
frozen in its skyward lunge;
a Himalayan Sufi temple of molten gold;
and a chain of three Gaudi stalagmites,
the ceiling of the cave rolled back,
the brush of sun and wind let in.

## *First Day in San Miguel de Allende*

I packed, of course, all the wrong
ideas, so had to rush out first thing
and buy clothes in warmer colours.
Only then could I hear the turtle doves,
the splash of fountain water over
ancient stone, see the bougainvillaea
scatter scarlet and cerise across the pilasters
of the Belles Artes courtyard arcade.

# To the Paddle Cactus

Plant world's fortress: Nopal—
self-contained and self-defending—
your spatulate, sharply whiskered scallops
displaced beaver tails
spiny and green and juice-filled. Edible.
Given to metastasis: one thumbless mitten
growing out of another until you stand
lop-sided, a stoic loner
adapted to sere, unsteady on your stem
but holding, close to your chest, a full house—
wax-museumed.

# Vesper
### Plaza de Allende, San Miguel, January 2001

At first in ones and twos,
then in droves, sleek-winged birds
clamour down from a sky
slowly draining of light. Evening
of the day after Three Kings' Day.
                    Little else changes,
but people begin to stroll
from under trees, vendors pack up sisal
mats, the moon's face
loses its pallor and sharpens.
                    The racket swells
as more and more boattail grackles
gather.  All screeching at once,
their shrieks merge into one
unnerving chord that's held
and held and held.
                    What needs saying
in this last hour?
                    Being unnerved can double
as comfort and I'm rapt up
out of myself in the black-feathered trees,
in a querulous commotion.
                    I know
it might not be this square, at the end,
but perhaps another with a formal garden,
its paths threading through bougainvillaea
and Japanese laurel, where townspeople,
accustomed to the black birds' strident ritual,
assemble and wait for dusk to fall
as evanescently as day's heat
leaves a stone wall and goes
                    where?

# *D* isharmony in Red

Red drenches the room, bled
                across table and walls, only window
and an empty chair
                untainted. And the woman
in black—head bowed
                over fruit in a bowl,
oblivious

                of the creeping disquiet, the thickening
vine.  Escaped from floral
                motif of tablecloth and *tapisserie*, it
serpents up, insurgent,
                into a forking like a buck's antlers
above the servant's head.  A proliferation—
                as in Gilman's story?—of tendrils,
like *an interminable string of toadstools*,
                *budding and sprouting in endless convolutions*
until they've caged, inside the wallpaper,
                a woman going mad?

Except in the orbs of fruit, Matisse has
                included no yellow, no foul, sulphurous
smell creeping through the house.
                And yet he painted into this painting
a window where no window was.

# *C*raving

Last night I ate bear.
Oh, it wasn't bear meat—
raw, fresh-frozen or cooked—
just two miniature bears carved
out of striated wood.  These
I swallowed whole—splinters
and all—off a tray in a shop
selling trinkets and toys. The dealer,
a woman I know but don't like,
wanted to charge more
than the two bric-a-brac bears were worth,
claiming both were plush teddies
and one held a fan (or was it a flag?)
but I knew what I'd eaten
so I contested the price
then swallowed my pride
and agreed to pay
by cheque as I had no cash.

# *C*redit River Gorge, Niagara Escarpment

The plume of water falls and falls again
into Ordovician and Silurian rock,
sandstone and shale from ancient seas—
four hundred million years of stone.

Into Ordovician and Silurian rock
epochs sediment and stratify—
four hundred million years of stone.
Sulphur butterflies flutter, weightless.

Epochs sediment and stratify.
Crab apples ripen in an abandoned orchard.
Sulphur butterflies flutter, weightless.
Queen Anne's Lace and clover ornament the path.

Crab apples ripen in an abandoned orchard.
Hillsides of sumac burst into flame.
Queen Anne's Lace and clover ornament the path.
A gulp, a gasp, the river surges forward.

Hillsides of sumac burst into flame.
Within a field of grass dog-day cicadas sing.
A gulp, a gasp, the river surges forward,
tumbling over the cliff in a taffeta swoon.

Within a field of grass dog-day cicadas sing.
Sandstone and shale from ancient seas.
Tumbling over the cliff in a taffeta swoon,
the plume of water falls and falls again.

# *U*p Tunnel Mountain Trail

Laboured, breathless, sweaty.  Exposed
roots like ropey veins on the back
of ageing hands. I pause to pant.  Up ahead
something small flitters and I see
a chipmunk stand up, strum the Pei Pa.  Sun
spangles the drugget of frost on pine needles
scattered like the pick-up-sticks of childhood.
Where do we get the notion that everything
will be all right in the end?  Grey flakes of bark
cling to the trunk of the dead still standing tree
I lean into, feel the brittle, rough rind,
wonder at the will to hold on, how my father
denied anything was wrong, tried to swim
a dozen laps though he'd twice choked
with that dread croaking sound.  At the summit
I breathe out into the encircling peaks three huge
OMs echoed by trucks crossing the valley,
while in my feet I feel the start
of the slip, the tumble down the mountain face,
hands clutching at roots, rocks,
straws.

## Before and After

Two faint barks
from a neighbourhood dog
tap my ear and recede
like the erratic
drip, drip
of a defective faucet,
then silence.
I brace myself
for the next but the next
doesn't come, and that
not-coming arrives
too late to ease my return
to where, in the dream,
I go through a door
I've gone through before.
Before and before.  Until after
a while, the befores far exceed
the what's-to-comes, stretching back
farther and farther but differently
from the way the future stretched ahead
like billowing hills, bluish
green and beckoning.

# Curved Mirrors

If true that the zebra finch
dreams of singing and sings in his dreams,
practising over and over, improvisatorially,

then dream is a place we take our daily experience
to rework and rehearse overnight
in preparation for tomorrow.

But also our anger and grief over the loss
of the squandered, the ruined; for the mind asleep,
some would say, is boundlessly protean,

both theatre and school, prescient
as well as preteritive. It feeds
on underground streams, divining what's to come

while enthralled in the what has been,
wandering among the curved
mirrors of the deeply remembered,

as if to live in dreams rather than the waking present
is to choose the already given over the not yet,
to look back as though already among the shades,

the arias of departed day.

# Withdrawn

How spend my days now I've days to spend?
Each night brings slight solace at lights out.
Living slows to a dawdle as it nears its end.

One falls inevitably behind the trends.
This year's tickets are all sold out.
How spend my days now I've days to spend?

Like a lending library with no books to lend,
I lack all means to relieve this drought.
Living slows to a dawdle as it nears its end.

Those urgent causes I fought to defend
have all dissolved into question, doubt.
How spend my days now I've days to spend?

Like a tamed animal who has ceased to fend,
I've ceased to care what the fuss is about.
Living slows to a dawdle as it nears its end.

Recalling the cadence of the willow's bend,
the quicksilver flash of a leaping trout
is how I spend days now I've days to spend.
Living slows to a dawdle as it nears its end.

# N*otes*

Epigraphs
> From James Marshall, *Pocketful of Nonsense.*
> From Steve Orlen, "Nature Rarely Confides in Me," in *This Particular Eternity*).
> From Aristotle, *On the Art of Poetry*, in T.S. Dorsch, trans. and ed., *Aristotle, Horace, Longinus: Classical Literary Criticism*).

*"le dernier sommeil"* (page 9-10)
> Inspired by the art installation "the final sleep—le dernier sommeil" by spring Hurlbut at the Royal Ontario Museum, April 28-August 12, 2001.

"Word Usage" (page 11)
> Quotation from Ivy Compton-Burnett, *Men & Wives* (1931), p. 151.

"The Thirteenth Element" (page 25)
> Based on Tim Flannery, "Glow in the Dark," review of *The 13th Element: The Sordid Tale of Murder, Fire, and Phosphorus*, by John Emsley, in *The New York Review of Books*, July 19, 2001 pp. 48, 50-52.

"The Grand Narrative" (page 28)
> Quotation from Jean-François Lyotard, *The Postmodern Condition: A Report on Knowledge* (1979/1984), 37.

"Post-war Photo" (page 38)
> Based on a photograph by Lee Miller.

"Ceremony" (page 40)
> is for Yuklin Renita Wong.

"Falling" (page 46)
> is for Thelma McCormack and Sylvia Van Kirk.

"Dreaming of this place" (page 47)
    is for Victor Belcher.

"Between Iola and Moran" (page 51)
    is for Mark Boyd.

"(Pender Island, April 16, 1997)" (pages 58-59)
    is for Marlene Cookshaw and Michael Kenyon.

"A Sonnenizio on a Line from Rilke" (page 60)
    Rainer Maria Rilke's "Sonnets to Orpheus," I, 3 A breath
    about nothing. A gust inside the god. A wind. Stephen
    Mitchell, trans. Invented by Kim Addonizio, a sonnenizio
    begins with a line from someone else's sonnet, takes a word
    from that line, and repeats it in each succeeding line of
    the 14-line poem.

"After a Poem by Paul Celan" (page 62)
    is a transposition of Paul Celan's poem "The Years From
    You To Me," Michael Hamburger, trans.

"Crossing the Steppes of Outer Mongolia" (pages 72-73)
    is for Daphne Marlatt.

"The Hoodoos" (page 74)
    is for Jaspreet Singh.

"Disharmony in Red" (page 78)
    Inspired by Matisse's painting "Harmony in Red (*la
    Desserte*)" (1908) and Charlotte Perkins Gilman, *The
    Yellow_Wallpaper* (1899).

# *Glossary*

*Altersheim*—old persons' home
*Apfelsine*—orange
*Aquarellen*—watercolours
*Ausrufezeichen*—exclamation marks

*Badewanne*—bathtub
*Blut und Boden*—blood and soil

*Einmarsch*—invasion
*entartet*—degenerate as in "*die entartete Kunst*," the so-called
"degenerate art" denounced and forbidden during the Nazi regime
*Ersatzkaffee*—coffee substitute
*Ersatzbutter*—butter substitute

*Gemälde*—painting
*Gipfel*—peak
*Großer Mohn*—Big Poppy

*Ein Hauch um Nichts. Ein Wehn im Gott. Ein Wind.*—A breath
about nothing. A gust inside the god. A wind.
*Hecke*—hedge
*Hof*—courtyard

*Ich weiß nicht, was soll es bedeuten,*
*Daß ich so traurig bin...*—"I know not what it means, that I am
so sad..." the opening lines of Heinrich Heine's poem "Die
Loreley"

*Jude*—jew

*Kaffeetrinken*—coffee-party
*Kampf*—fight, struggle, battle
*Kartoffeln*—potatoes
*Kaufhaus*—department store
*Kronprinz*—crown prince

*Kuchen*—cake
*KZ*—common abbreviation for *Konzentrationslager*, concentration camp

*Liebe*—love

*Meckerziegenschwester*—bleating goat sister
*Mutti*—mommy

*Nachlaß*—legacy

*saftig*—juicy
*Satz*—sentence
*Schwierigkeiten*—difficulties
*Schwung*—swing, momentum

*die Tauben*—the doves
*der Tod ist ein Meister aus Deutschland*—"death is a master from Germany," oft-quoted line from Paul Celan's poem "*Todesfuge*" ("Death Fugue")

*ungemalte Bilder*—unpainted pictures

*Vati*—daddy
*verboten*—forbidden
*verrecke!*—die (of cattle and, vulgarly, of people)
*das Volk*—the folk, the people

*Die Wacht am Rhein*—"The Watch on the Rhine," the title of a well-known German nationalistic song

*Waschlappen*—washcloth
*Weberstraße*—Weber Street

*Zehennägel*—toenails
*zick, zack*—zig, zag